IRISH FOLK
WISDOM

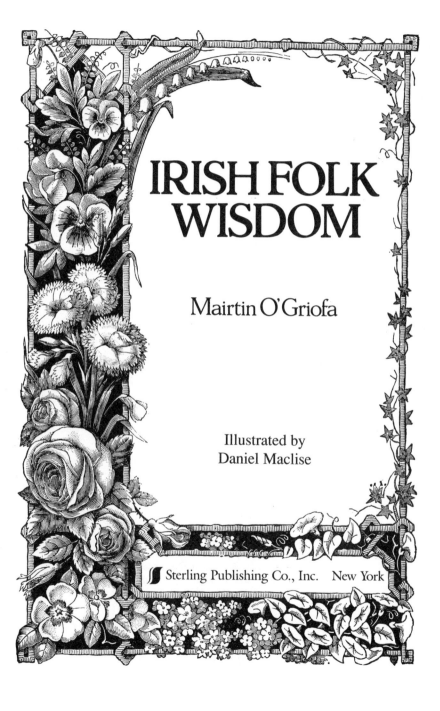

IRISH FOLK WISDOM

Mairtin O'Griofa

Illustrated by
Daniel Maclise

Sterling Publishing Co., Inc.   New York

Library of Congress Cataloging-in-Publication Data.

O'Griofa, Mairtin.
      Irish Folk Wisdom / Mairtin O'Griofa.
         p.   cm.
      Includes index.
      ISBN 0-8069-0379-1
        1. Folklore—Ireland. 2. Proverbs, Irish. 3. Ireland—Social
life and customs. I. Title.
      GR153.5.034 1993
      398.2'09415—dc20   92-45750
                                                CIP

10 9 8 7 6 5 4 3 2

Published by Sterling Publishing Company, Inc.
387 Park Avenue South, New York, N.Y. 10016
© 1993 by Sterling Publishing Company, Inc.
Distributed in Canada by Sterling Publishing
c/o Canadian Manda Group, P.O. Box 920, Station U
Toronto, Ontario, Canada M8Z 5P9
Distributed in Great Britain and Europe by Cassell PLC
Villiers House, 41/47 Strand, London WC2N 5JE, England
Distributed in Australia by Capricorn Link Ltd.
P.O. Box 665, Lane Cove, NSW 2066
Manufactured in the United States of America
All rights reserved

Sterling ISBN 0-8069-0379-1

For Sally

Slán agat a mhadra dhílis uasal,
faoin bhfód id' luí,
go gcónaí tú sa tsíocháin

Contents

Introduction   9

The Animal Kingdom   13
Love and Marriage   37
House and Hearth, Food and Drink   49
God, Church, and the Devil   61
Matters of Life and Death   65
Rich and Poor, Friend and Neighbor   73
Wise Man and Fool   81
Luck and Misfortune   87
Toil and Labor   93
Triads   99
Words to the Wise   109

Index   127

Introduction

The folk wisdom of any nation is recorded in its proverbs, and, as almost everyone knows, a proverb is a short statement of wisdom or advice which has passed through the years into general use. More homely than aphorisms, proverbs generally refer to common experience and are often expressed in metaphor, alliteration, or rhyme, e.g., "Don't scald your lips on another person's porridge" (metaphor) or "Health is better than wealth" (rhyme). The frequent dependence on alliteration and rhyme, in fact, makes it difficult to translate these proverbial nuggets of wisdom from one language to another. The many proverbs in this book translated from the original Irish will therefore rarely match the alliterative poetry of the originals, but will in every case capture the full measure of metaphoric meaning.

Nearly every nation has its store of proverbs, though many are common to several nations. There are within Irish folk wisdom proverbs original to the Irish language, proverbs translated into Irish from those of English settlers, proverbs adapted from those in the Bible and in ancient and modern languages, and those that originated in modern Anglo-Irish times. Sometimes it is difficult to know the specific origins of what is now collectively considered Irish folk wisdom. Examples of both ancient and modern Irish proverbs are included in the present collection.

There is no surer sign of the oral knowledge of a people being on the wane than the attempt to rescue it from oblivion by recollecting its fragments and putting them in books. With modern Ireland in transition and becoming more and more like its European neighbors by the day, transmission of proverbial speech from mouth to mouth— "on the living voices of the people"—ceases to be the rule. Today transmission, incision, and fruition in such matters depend on the written or printed word, figure, or date. If there is one medium more than another that will perpetuate for us the wit and wisdom of our Irish ancestors, who belonged to a time when mother wit and native shrewdness took the place of present-day sharpness, that medium is the proverb.

"Our proverbs," wrote one early observer, "truly portray the character of Irish people as a mixture of diverse qualities, some admirable, some not so, but on the whole very respectable, seldom repulsive, oftener attractive, and rarely indicating selfishness, stupidity, heartlessness, or treachery. Indeed, such faults are repeatedly reproved in our proverbs with antipathy, contempt, and abhorrence. On the other hand, all the virtues of Truthfulness, Honesty, Fidelity, Self-restraint, Self-esteem, Sense of Honor, Courage, Caution, Generosity, Hospitality, Courtesy, Peaceableness, Love of Kindred, Patience, Promptness,

Industry, and Providence are highly commended." Despite the seriousness of its subject matter, a vein of quiet humor runs throughout Irish folk wisdom.

Like all nations, Ireland has many proverbs attempting to portray the "inscrutable" ways of women. A good number of these proverbs, their humorous intent notwithstanding, will seem tasteless and offensive to many modern readers, but to exclude them from a representative anthology of Irish folk wisdom would falsify history. The status of women in today's Ireland is rapidly changing, as elsewhere in the West, but the war between the sexes remains prevalent in what is still very much a man's world. Whatever the old attitudes to women, the sacredness of marriage, parental control, and the dutiful rearing of offspring— homilies for the education of the child, and for the conduct of the adult, between person and person and between the individual and the community, are given in that terse and effective language so characteristic of Irish folk wisdom.

Most modern anthologies of Irish proverbs and sayings translated into English build, to some degree, on several early collections, including Mícheál Óg Ó Longáin's collection of c. 1800, one of the earliest. Others essential to any anthology in English include T. F. O'Rahilly's *A Miscellany of Irish Proverbs* (1922), T. D. MacDonald's *Gaelic Proverbs and Proverbial Sayings* (1926), and an anonymous collection, published in London in 1913 and unusually modern for its day, entitled *National Proverbs: Ireland*. P. W. Joyce's *English as We Speak It in Ireland* (1910), though obviously not an anthology, contains many Irish proverbs not found in other sources. A unique source of thousands of animal proverbs is A. R. Forbes's *Gaelic Names of Beasts (Mammalia), Birds, Fishes, Insects, Reptiles, etc.,* privately printed in 1905 and consequently available in only a small number of libraries. Of collections intended for the modern reader, the best include *Proverbs & Sayings of Ireland,* edited by Sean Gaffney and Seamus Cashman (Dublin, 1974) and *The Poolbeg Book of Irish Proverbs,* compiled by Fionnuala Williams (Swords, Co. Dublin, 1992). The latter is rich in manuscript material, newly translated from the Irish, in the collections of the Department of Irish Folklore, University College, Dublin.

The illustrations in this book are by the Irish artist Daniel Maclise. Born in Cork in 1806, Maclise was discovered by Sir Walter Scott on a visit to that city when the young artist did a very successful sketch of the writer, was befriended by him, and urged to study painting in London. Although Maclise is remembered mainly for his series of portrait drawings of eminent Victorian writers, including his lifelong friend Charles Dickens, and for his famous frescoes in the House of Lords, his interest in Irish subjects, particularly Celtic mythology, never flagged. Several of Maclise's illustrations from Irish myths are included in the pages that follow.

THE ANIMAL KINGDOM

D. Maclise, R.A.

F. Joubert.

Asses

Hurry no man's cattle — get a jackass for yourself.

———— * ————

Better an ass that carries you than a horse that throws you.

———— * ————

Put an ass to grass and it will still come home an ass.

———— * ————

A hungry ass keeps his kicking end down.

———— * ————

The good speech of an ass is better than the bad word of a prophet.

———— * ————

An ass never goes bald.

Badgers

'Tis the badger that is quickest to feel its own smell.

Bulls

A town without a landlord or a bull goes topsy turvy.

———— * ————

Take the bull to the mansion and it will go to the byre.

CALVES

Be it fat or lean, pity the man that won't rear a calf for himself.

———— * ————

Grass that hasn't grown will suit the unborn calf.

———— * ————

One calf is better than two skins.

———— * ————

Many things befall the calf that his dam never thought of.

———— * ————

The calf's skin often goes to market before his mother's.

———— * ————

Smooth is the calf that his mother licks.

CATS

What can you expect from a cat but her skin?

———— * ————

It's to please herself that the cat purrs.

———— * ————

If the cat had a churn, her paw would often be in it.

———— * ————

Too many cats are worse than rats.

———— * ————

What would a young cat do but kill a mouse?

———— * ————

A man who is idle will put the cat on the fire.

———— * ————

The cat's milk makes no cream.

———— * ————

Cats never do good but in spite of themselves.

———— * ————

Nature shines through the cat's eyes.

———— * ————

An old cat won't burn himself.

———— * ————

It's not good to be telling lies, as the cat said when the wolf ate him.

———— * ————

The cat's leavings are fit only for himself.

———— * ————

It's not easy to put pants on a cat.

———— * ————

What could a cat bring forth but kittens?

———— * ————

If the cat sits long enough at the hole, she will catch the mouse.

———— * ————

Who knows best to take the cat out of the churn but he that put her in?

———— * ————

Combat the cat and it will bristle up.

———— * ————

Every cat is gray at night.

———— * ————

The tail is part of the cat.

———— * ————

Send not the cat for suet.

———— * ————

The cats would do well till the mice would take their ears off.

———— * ————

The cat may look at the king, but the king may put the eyes out of the cat.

———— * ————

17

The cat wonders at its having a tail.

Cows

Out of her head the cow is milked.

———— * ————

Far-off cows have long horns.

———— * ————

One who is cowless must be his own dog.

[A poor man must forage for himself.]

———— * ————

Show the fatted calf but not the thing that fattened him.

———— * ————

In winter the milk goes to the cow's horns.

———— * ————

A bad cow is better than none.

———— * ————

The leanest cow in the fold lows the loudest.

———— * ————

Shun a cow's horn and a horse's hinder parts.

———— * ————

One cow breaks the fence, and a dozen leap it.

———— * ————

Cows wear with milking.

———— * ————

A cow is only a good deal bigger than the midge.

———— * ————

You can't sell the cow and drink her milk.

———— * ————

All the cows do not come equally to the fold.

———— * ————

The cow can give her calf only what she has.

———— * ————

What would you expect from a cow but a moo?

———— * ————

I'd rather have the cow that would fill a thimble than one that would fill a churn and spill it.

———— * ————

Where a cow is, a woman will be.

———— * ————

The man of one cow must twist her tail round his fist.

[He must look well after her.]

———— * ————

The low is greater than the milking.

———— * ————

Better have no cow than no son.

———— * ————

A starved cow never fills the pail.

———— * ————

One living teat is better than two dead cows.

———— * ————

The cow is the first to notice her own calf.

———— * ————

Many a good cow has had a bad calf.

———— * ————

A hornless cow likes another hornless cow.

———— * ————

One cow will spoil a fold.

———— * ————

Do not take a cow from a gardener.

[It will likely be difficult to keep.]

Deer

Food will tame the mountain deer.

———— * ————

The swiftness of the roe is known without the loosing of the hounds.

———— * ————

The fawn is swifter than its mother.

———— * ————

The older the buck, the harder his horn.

———— * ————

Don't skin the deer till you get it.

Dogs

Hit a dog with a bone and he won't growl.

———— * ————

Quarrelsome dogs get dirty coats.

———— * ————

The hungry hound thinks not of her whelps.

———— * ————

It's hard to teach an old dog to dance.

———— * ————

One dog will cause all the others to bark.

———— * ————

Be good to the dog and he will follow you.

———— * ————

A full dog won't hunt.

———— * ————

A dead dog won't bark.

———— * ————

The moon is none the worse of the dogs barking at her.

———— * ————

There is no fight like the old dog's fight.

———— * ————

A starving dog gets no bone.

[He that hath will get.]

There never was a swift dog that didn't get its fill of work.

———— * ————

An old dog cannot change his way of barking.

———— * ————

A dog won't howl at a bone.

———— * ————

Turn out the Englishman and bring in the dog.

———— * ————

A dog may have a spirit as well as a man.

———— * ————

A dog's caution is in his feet.

———— * ————

If the cat scratches you, don't beat the dog.

———— * ————

A dog's grin is just like an Englishman's laugh.

———— * ————

Far will a masterless dog travel.

———— * ————

A dog's leavings are better than a fool's.

———— * ————

One dog fleeing is swifter than twelve pursuing.

———— * ————

It's hard to choose between two blind dogs.

———— * ————

If you put your hand in a dog's mouth, you must take it out
as best you can.

———— * ————

The dog that fetches will carry.

———— * ————

Follow a dog and he will not bite you.

———— * ————

A bad name kills dogs.

Do not throw stones at a dead dog.

———— * ————

A well-trained dog goes out when he knows he's about to be thrown out.

———— * ————

The more a dog gets the more he wants.

———— * ————

If I say "get out" to my dog, everybody will say it.

———— * ————

A house without a dog is a house without laughter.

———— * ————

Playing with a pup ends in a howl.

———— * ————

Better the dog that dips its tail than the dog that snarls.

———— * ————

Every dog is bold on its own dunghill.

———— * ————

A dog is the better off for another dog being reproved.

———— * ————

What can you expect from a dog but a bite?

———— * ————

If you strike a dog or a lout, strike home.

———— * ————

It's an ill dog that is not worth the whistling.

———— * ————

A slow hound is often lucky.

———— * ————

Better to have a dog fawn on you than bark at you.

———— * ————

Every hound is a pup until he hunts.

DONKEYS

Every time a donkey brays, an Irishman dies.

FOXES

The fox never found a better messenger than himself.

———— * ————

The fox will go no farther than his feet will carry him.

———— * ————

It's a fine day when the fox turns preacher.

———— * ————

He who would cheat the fox must rue early.

———— * ————

Even his own tail is a burden to the [weary] fox.

———— * ————

If the fox runs into the hound's embrace, who's to blame?

———— * ————

The older the worse — like the fox's cubs.

———— * ————

In spite of the fox's cunning, his skin is often sold.

GOATS

It's no use going to the goat's house to look for wool.

———— * ————

Do not mistake a goat's beard for a fine stallion's tail.

———— * ————

If you see a goat, hit him because he's either getting into
mischief or just getting out of it.

———— * ————

Women have goats' eyes in keeping their husbands to
themselves.

[Goats are very keen-eyed.]

If you put a silk suit on a goat, it is still a goat.

———— * ————

Only sickness would keep goats from eating ivy

———— * ————

It is natural for the kid to bleat.

———— * ————

The kid will soon be worse than the old buck.

———— * ————

The goats will be deaf at harvest time.

———— * ————

Men have goats' eyes in choosing their wives.

HORSES

Forgive a horse that'll cock his ears.

———— * ————

The losing horse blames the saddle.

———— * ————

Many a shabby colt makes a fine horse.

———— * ————

It's easy to see a white horse in a bog.

———— * ————

Everyone lays a burden on the willing horse.

———— * ————

Even a good horse cannot keep running forever.

———— * ————

A nod is as good as a wink to a blind horse.

———— * ————

An old mare's foal will never come to much.

———— * ————

He that buys an old hack will have to buy another horse.

———— * ————

It is easy to ride with your own whip and another's horse.

The horse that is struck on the head will be timid thereafter.

———— * ————

When you mount your high horse, you tumble over it.

———— * ————

A borrowed horse never tires.

———— * ————

A woman's horse won't do plowing.

———— * ————

It's hard to stop an old horse from kicking.

———— * ————

The willing horse ought not to be urged.

———— * ————

It is no shame to a man to be thrown by a mare.

———— * ————

An old horse needs fresh grass.

———— * ————

Nobody knows where the white horses come from.

———— * ————

Horse first, wife last.

———— * ————

An old horse may neigh.

———— * ————

Though the man is the farmer, the horse is the laborer.

———— * ————

You can't judge a horse by his harness.

———— * ————

An inch of a horse is better than a foot of a mare.

———— * ————

A good horse may be forgiven a kick.

———— * ————

Often it's not the best horse that wins the race.

———— * ————

It's a good horse that pulls its own load.

If you have a halter, you'll get a horse.

———— * ————

One nail will spoil the horse, and one horse will spoil the team.

———— * ————

Even the four-footed horse may stumble.

———— * ————

The slow horse will reach the mill, but the one that breaks its bones will not.

LIONS

Every man is a lion over what's his own.

———— * ————

The lion is known by the scratch of his claw.

MICE

What is silent the mice won't hear.

———— * ————

The little mouse is mistress in her own house.

———— * ————

A mouse is bold under a haystack.

MULES

A mule is more obstinate than the devil, but a woman is more obstinate than a mule.

OXEN

There's another turn in the ox's horn.

PIGS

If I like the sow, I like her litter.

———— * ————

The miller's pigs are fat, but God knows whose meal they ate.

———— * ————

A person that's made a pet of and a pig that's made a pet of are the two worst pets of all.

———— * ————

Pigs won't thrive on clean water.

———— * ————

It's not the pick of the swine that the beggar gets.

———— * ————

From the sow comes but a little pig.

———— * ————

It's not the big sow that eats the most.

———— * ————

Even the sow will keep her own sty clean.

———— * ————

It's on the fat pig the butter goes.

[He that has gets.]

———— * ————

As a jewel in a pig's snout is a woman without understanding.

———— * ————

A thieving pig's ear can hear the grass growing.

———— * ————

It is not the quietest sow that eats the least.

———— * ————

Catch the pig by the leg when you can.

Rabbits

One bite of a rabbit is worth two of a cat.

———— * ————

It is hard to drive a hare out of a bush in which he is not.

[Said of attempting the impossible.]

Rats

The last kick of a dying rat is always the worst.

Seals

The young seal takes naturally to the sea.

———— * ————

A seal is swifter than a mackerel.

Sheep

There was never a scabby sheep in a flock that didn't like to have a comrade.

———— * ————

You might as well hang for a sheep as for a goat.

———— * ————

In spring when the sheep is lean, shellfish are fat.

———— * ————

A white sheep may have a black lamb, and a black sheep a white one.

———— * ————

The ragged sheep that goes into the briars will leave her wool there.

———— * ————

Tethered sheep will not thrive.

———— * ————

The sheep's jaw will put the plow on the henhouse.

[Sheep farming will drive out agriculture.]

———— * ————

If one sheep puts his head through the gap, the rest will follow.

———— * ————

If the brier were not in the way, the sheep would not go into it.

———— * ————

One cannot tell whether the skin of the old sheep or of the young sheep will be the sooner suspended on the rafter.

———— * ————

A lamb when carried far becomes as burdensome as a sheep.

Wolves

When you go a-visiting the wolf, take your dog with you.

Birds

The silly bird's foot will go into the snare.

———— * ————

Birds do not light on only one branch.

———— * ————

Where the fish is, there the birds will be.

———— * ————

Every bird according to his rearing.

———— * ————

Though the egg be small, a bird will come out of it.

———— * ————

Sweet sings each bird in its own grove.

———— * ————

The hungry bird fights best.

———— * ————

The birds are good in their native place.

———— * ————

If the bird be flown, the nest may burn.

———— * ————

Don't say "chuck" to the chick until it is out of the egg.

———— * ————

Take a bird out of a clean nest.

[Refers to the selection of a husband or wife.]

———— * ————

Bit by bit the bird builds her nest.

CHICKENS

As the old cock crows, so the young bird chirrups.

———— * ————

Loud cackle, little egg.

———— * ————

A dead hen is done laying.

———— * ————

The chicken that will come out of a cock's egg can destroy
the world.

———— * ————

'Tis not common for hens to have pillows.

———— * ————

A laying hen is better than a nest of eggs.

———— * ————

A black hen will lay a white egg.

———— * ————

The hen is very bountiful with the horse's corn.

———— * ————

It's a bad hen that can't scratch for herself.

You can't expect a big egg from a little hen.

———— * ————

The scraping hen will get something, but the crouching hen will get nothing.

———— * ————

The sitting hen never fattens.

———— * ————

The cock is a good timepiece.

———— * ————

A hen carried far is heavy.

———— * ————

The cocks crow but the hens lay the eggs.

———— * ————

A dead cock cannot crow.

CROWS

Wherever the crow goes she'll take her tail with her.

———— * ————

It is in the evening the crow makes water.

———— * ————

A crow won't caw without a reason.

DOVES

The higher the dove goes, the likelier is the hawk to catch it.

DUCKS

It's natural for ducks to go barefoot.

GEESE

Even the geese understand each other.

Don't pluck your goose until you catch her.

———— * ————

A wild goose never laid a tame egg.

———— * ————

Those who have a goose will get a goose.

HAWKS

You cannot make hawks of kites.

———— * ————

The hawk's eyes are in the heads of women when choosing
a husband.

———— * ————

A closed hand catches no hawk.

KITES

A clean bird never came out of a kite's nest.

———— * ————

It's not for nought that the kite whistles.

LARKS

There is no smoke in the lark's house.

RAVENS

The raven that rises early gets the eye of the beast in the
bog.

[i.e., a dainty, a treat.]

———— * ————

Even the ravens must live.

———— * ————

The raven thinks its own chick the prettiest.

Swallows

You can't teach a swallow to fly.

Wrens

The wren spreads his feet wide in his own home.
[Even the most insignificant are kings in their castles.]

———— * ————

'Tis the less for that, 'tis the less for that, as the wren said
when it sipped a billful out of the sea.

———— * ————

It's the bigger of that, it's the bigger of that, as the wren
said when it pissed in the sea.

———— * ————

A wren in the hand is better than a crane to be caught.

———— * ————

Although the wren is small, it will make a noise.

Fish

The fish that bites every worm will be caught in time.

———— * ————

Dry shoes won't get fish.

———— * ————

There are finer fish in the sea than have ever been caught.

———— * ————

Where the fish is the birds will be.

———— * ————

A little fish is better than no fish at all.

———— * ————

Do not bless the fish until it is landed.

Herrings

Let every herring hang by its own tail.

Lobsters

Better a lobster than no husband.

[Said by a woman who placed a live lobster in her bag of potatoes to detect a thief.]

Salmon

There's no salmon without peer.

Shellfish

A hasty foot won't get shellfish.

———— * ————

It's a bare stone where no shellfish are to be found.

Trout

Listen for the flood of the river and you'll catch a trout.

Insects and Reptiles

An ant has only to look on an eagle to know its own insignificance.

———— * ————

A tiny bee can make a large cow gad.

———— * ————

One beetle knows another.

———— * ————

A fly is of little account until it gets into the eye.

———— * ————

The fly that rises from the dunghill makes the loudest hum.

[Refers to the boastfulness of the self-made man.]

———— * ————

Every little frog is great in his own bog.

———— * ————

When a sharp point pierces the frog, it shrieks.

———— * ————

You can't pluck a frog.

———— * ————

'Tis not where water is a frog will be, but where a frog is
water will be.

LOVE AND MARRIAGE

D. Maclise, R.A.

WOMEN

It's as hard to see a woman crying as it is to see a barefoot duck.

———— * ————

A dishonest woman can't be kept in and an honest woman won't.

———— * ————

A Tyrone woman will never buy a rabbit without a head for fear it's a cat.

———— * ————

Women are stronger than men; they do not die of wisdom.

———— * ————

There is nothing more wicked than a woman of evil temper.

———— * ————

The mother's failings will naturally be seen in the daughter.

———— * ————

A bad woman knows a foolish man's faults.

———— * ————

A red-haired black-eyed woman; a dun fiery-eyed dog; a black-haired red-bearded man—the three unluckiest to meet.

———— * ————

There never was good or ill without a woman being concerned in it.

———— * ————

A bad woman drinks a lot of her own bad buttermilk.

———— * ————

Where there's a cow there will be a woman, and where there's a woman there will be trouble.

———— * ————

A whistling woman and a crowing hen will bring no luck to the house they are in.

———— * ————

Woman's patience — till you count three!

———— * ————

She is beef to the heels like a Mullingar heifer.

———— * ————

Meal is finer than grain, women are finer than men.

———— * ————

Eight lives for the men and nine for the women.

———— * ————

Woman was God's second mistake.

———— * ————

Modesty is the beauty of women.

———— * ————

Where there are women there's talking, and where there's geese there's cackling.

———— * ————

A cow will spoil a fold; a woman will spoil a township.

———— * ————

Irish women have a dispensation from the Pope to wear the thick ends of their legs downwards.

———— * ————

Three things you cannot comprehend: the mind of a woman, the working of the bees, and the ebb and flow of the tide.

————— * —————

Women are shy, and shame prevents them from refusing a
man.

————— * —————

The nature of a hen, of a sow, and of a woman —to have
her own way.

————— * —————

Everything dear is a woman's fancy.

————— * —————

One woman understands another.

————— * —————

Teaching a turbulent woman is like strokes of a hammer on
cold iron.

————— * —————

She would drink the cream and say the cat she had was an
old rogue.

————— * —————

Like an Irish wolf she barks at her own shadow.

————— * —————

The daughter of an active old woman makes a bad
housekeeper.

————— * —————

More hair than tit, like a mountain heifer.

————— * —————

The three most pleasant things—a cat's kitten, a goat's kid,
and a young widow.

————— * —————

When the old woman is hard-pressed, she has to run.

————— * —————

There are three without rule—a mule, a pig, and a woman.

————— * —————

It's difficult to trust a woman.

A man without a woman is like a neck without a pain.

———— * ————

The beauty of a chaste woman makes bitter words.

———— * ————

Men to the hills, women to the shore.

———— * ————

Irish beauty—a woman with two black eyes.

———— * ————

Only a fool would prefer food to a woman.

———— * ————

Donegal girls, who are redheaded and therefore strong-smelling, are said to be born with a pig under the bed.

———— * ————

There are three kinds of men who fail to understand women — young men, old men, and middle-aged men.

———— * ————

Beat a woman with a hammer and you'll have gold.

———— * ————

A shrew will get her wish though her soul will not get mercy.

———— * ————

An excuse is nearer to a woman than her apron.

———— * ————

There is nothing sharper than a woman's tongue.

———— * ————

A woman can beat the devil.

LOVE

What is nearest the heart is nearest the lips.

———— * ————

Live in my heart and pay no rent.

I love you—and what you have.

———— * ————

They won't fall in love with the man they don't see.

———— * ————

Constant gazing betokens love.

———— * ————

Love is blind to blemishes and fault.

———— * ————

Love a dunghill and you'll see no motes in it.

———— * ————

When the sight leaves the eye, love leaves the heart.

———— * ————

After the dowry comes the love.

———— * ————

Courting is a costly mistress.

———— * ————

She who fills the heart fills the eye.

———— * ————

Love is no impartial judge.

———— * ————

He who dotes in the dark sees no motes.

———— * ————

Love conceals ugliness, and hate sees many faults.

MARRIAGE

Court abroad but marry at home.

———— * ————

There is no cure for love but marriage.

———— * ————

There never was an old slipper but there was an old
stocking to match it.

———— * ————

A poor man must have a poor wedding.

———— * ————

Woe to him who does not heed a good wife's counsel.

———— * ————

Many an Irish property was increased by the lace of a daughter's petticoat.

———— * ————

The husband of the sloven is known in the field amidst a crowd.

———— * ————

Marriages are all happy; it's having breakfast together that causes all the problems.

———— * ————

Young man, you'll be troubled till you marry, and from then on you'll never have rest.

———— * ————

A growing moon and a flowing tide are lucky times to marry.

———— * ————

The carefree mother's daughter makes a bad wife.

———— * ————

A bad wife takes advice from everyone but her own husband.

———— * ————

Never make a toil of pleasure, as the man said when he dug his wife's grave only three feet deep.

———— * ————

The lying man's witness is his wife.

———— * ————

There's only one thing on earth better than a good wife, and that's no wife.

———— * ————

There are no trials until one gets married.

He breaks his wife's head and then buys a bandage for it.

———— * ————

The shoemaker's wife and the smith's mare often go barefoot.

———— * ————

A ring on the finger and not a stitch of clothes on the back.

———— * ————

Anything is better than a bad marriage.

———— * ————

The blanket is the warmer for being doubled.

———— * ————

Marry in haste and be sorry in leisure.

———— * ————

He who marries a wife marries trouble.

———— * ————

Every man can rule a shrew except the one she's married to.

———— * ————

He married money and got a woman with it.

———— * ————

There's no feast until a roast and no torment until a marriage.

———— * ————

Better a wise wife than a plow and land.

———— * ————

Worst of fuel, alder green; worst thing human, malice keen; worst of drink, wine without life, but worst of all, a bad wife.

———— * ————

Marry a mountainy woman and you'll marry the mountain.

———— * ————

There'll be white blackbirds before an unwilling woman marries.

Take no woman for a wife who presents herself without a flaw.

———— * ————

The day you marry your wife you marry your children.

———— * ————

If you marry at all, marry last year.

———— * ————

It's a lonesome washing without a man's shirt in it.

———— * ————

If you wish to be praised, die; if you wish to be decried, marry.

———— * ————

Choose not the smooth-tongued one, the grinning one, or the squint-eyed one; but the little sallow mouse-colored one, neither seek nor shun her.

[In short, don't marry.]

———— * ————

Do not take a wife from a mansion or a cow from a gardener.

———— * ————

I married a trollop for her gear; her gear is gone, but she's still here.

———— * ————

Marriage will sober love.

———— * ————

Choose your wife with her nightcap on.

———— * ————

What's all the world to a man when his wife is a widow?

CHILDREN

A son like the mother, and a daughter like the father.

———— * ————

Praise the child and it will progress.

———— * ————

The unfortunate only son naturally goes to the dogs.

———— * ————

If children won't make you laugh, they won't make you cry.

———— * ————

The child that's left to himself will put his mother to shame.

———— * ————

Baptize you own child first.

———— * ————

A child will be known by its manners.

———— * ————

A wise son makes a father glad, but a foolish son is a mother's sorrow.

———— * ————

A woman may bear a son, but God makes the heir.

———— * ————

What the child sees is what the child does.

———— * ————

The feeding of a growing boy would a grain mill aye employ.

———— * ————

An inch of a lad is better than a foot of a girl.

———— * ————

A light-heeled mother makes a leaden-heeled daughter.

———— * ————

If you love the mother, you love her brood.

———— * ————

A boy's best friend is his mother, and there's no spancel stronger than her apron string.

———— * ————

Every finger has not the same length, nor every son the
same disposition.

———— * ————

A supple mother makes a lazy child.

———— * ————

Your son is your son today, but your daughter is your
daughter forever.

———— * ————

Every mother thinks it's for her own child the sun rises.

———— * ————

No man ever wore a tie as nice as his child's arm around
his neck.

———— * ————

There's no love until there's a family.

———— * ————

HOUSE AND HEARTH
FOOD AND DRINK

HOUSE AND HEARTH

There's no hearth like your own hearth.

———— * ————

Wide is the door of the little cottage.

———— * ————

A hut is a palace to a poor man.

———— * ————

Possession satisfies.

———— * ————

The eye should be blind in the house of another.

———— * ————

A little fire that warms is better than a big fire that burns.

———— * ————

Firelight will not let you read fine stories, but it's warm and you won't see the dust on the floor.

———— * ————

The old pipe gives the sweetest smoke.

———— * ————

It's a long way from home that the plover cries.

———— * ————

Keep your house and your house will keep you.

———— * ————

Dirty hands make a clean hearth.

Don't burn your fingers when you have tongs.

———— * ————

A new broom sweeps clean, but an old one knows the dirty corners best.

———— * ————

See that your own hearth is swept before you lift your neighbor's ashes.

———— * ————

Fire is a good servant, but a bad master.

———— * ————

Silk and satin and scarlet leave a fireless, colorless hearth.

———— * ————

Sweep the corners; the middle will sweep itself.

———— * ————

Even a tin knocker will shine on a dirty door.

———— * ————

He who is bad at giving a lodging is good at showing the road.

———— * ————

A windy day is not the day for thatching.

———— * ————

It is easier to demolish a house than to build one.

FOOD

Hunger is a good sauce.

———— * ————

A ha'porth of 'taties and a farthing's worth of fat will make a good dinner for an Irish Pat.

———— * ————

Good humor comes from the kitchen.

———— * ————

You don't know what's in the pot until the lid is lifted.

No fumes from the pot, but from what it contains.

———— * ————

All living creatures must be fed.

———— * ————

'Tis pleasant with company at the table; woe to him who eats alone.

———— * ————

Taste the food and you'll get a taste for it.

———— * ————

Help is a good thing except at the dinner table.

———— * ————

Food is a workhorse.

———— * ————

He's first at the pot and last at the work.

———— * ————

He's a man at the food and a weakling at the work.

———— * ————

The juice of the cow alive or dead is good.

———— * ————

The man who has butter gets more butter.

———— * ————

Just as the day broke, butter broke.

———— * ————

Though honey is sweet, do not lick it off a briar.

———— * ————

No feast till there is the roast.

———— * ————

It's easy to bake when the meal's beside you.

———— * ————

Where there's meal there's bound to be salt.

———— * ————

The man who has bread will find a knife to cut it.

Eaten bread is soon forgotten.

———— * ————

You've got the hiccup from the bread and butter you never ate.

———— * ————

A clean fast is better than a dirty breakfast.

———— * ————

When all fruit fails, welcome haws.

———— * ————

Never scald your lips on another man's porridge.

———— * ————

You look for the ladle when the pot's on the fire.

———— * ————

Let broth boil slowly, but let porridge make a noise.

———— * ————

The first drop of the broth is the hottest.

———— * ————

You can't eat soup with a fork.

———— * ————

A trout in the pot is better than a salmon in the sea.

———— * ————

A stew boiled is a stew spoiled.

———— * ————

It's no use boiling your cabbage twice.

———— * ————

You must crack the nut before you can eat the kernel.

———— * ————

The only cure for spilled milk is to lick the pitcher.

———— * ————

I think little of buttermilk when I'm full of it.

———— * ————

He is like the bagpipes; he never makes a noise till his belly's full.

When the belly is full, the bones like to stretch.

———— * ————

Tobacco after food.

DRINK

Who drinks only water never gets drunk.

———— * ————

Wine is old men's milk.

———— * ————

Wine drowns more men than water.

———— * ————

Wine is better than blood.

———— * ————

Sweet is the wine but sour's the payment.

———— * ————

Drink is the curse of the land. It makes you fight with your neighbor, it makes you shoot at your landlord, and it makes you miss.

———— * ————

A narrow neck keeps the bottle from being emptied in one swig.

———— * ————

What butter and whiskey won't cure there's no cure for.

———— * ————

It's the first drop that destroyed me; there's no harm at all in the last.

———— * ————

It'd make a rabbit spit at a dog.

[Said of strong whiskey.]

———— * ————

It's nothing but folly to treat an old woman to a dram.

———— * ————

He'd go to mass every morning if holy water were whiskey.

———— * ————

Send round the glass to the south, from the left to the right hand, all things should front the south.

———— * ————

A drink is shorter than a story.

———— * ————

Do not be talkative in an alehouse.

———— * ————

Drunkenness and anger speak truth.

———— * ————

A drunken woman is lost to shame.

———— * ————

Chose your company before you drink.

———— * ————

You take your health once too often to the whiskey shop till it gets broken.

———— * ————

It's sweet to drink but bitter to pay for it.

———— * ————

Thirst after the drink and sorrow after the money.

———— * ————

When good luck comes the drink comes.

———— * ————

Thirst begets thirst.

———— * ————

Drunkenness will not protect a secret.

———— * ————

The end of drinking is more thirst.

———— * ————

The cure of the drinking is to drink again.

The inebriated heart will not lie.

———— * ————

Wine is the best liquor to wash glasses in.

———— * ————

Drink as much after an egg as after an ox.

———— * ————

Wine makes old women wenches.

———— * ————

Take a drink with your porridge and you'll cough in your grave.

———— * ————

The more you drink the more you may.

———— * ————

Wine and women empty men's pockets.

———— * ————

Drink well is eat well's brother.

GOD, CHURCH
AND THE DEVIL

GOD

God's help is nearer than the door.

———— * ————

When God comes in the door, the devil flies out the window.

———— * ————

God is not as severe as He is said to be.

———— * ————

God fits the back to suit the burden.

———— * ————

God often pays debts without money.

———— * ————

God is good till morning.

———— * ————

God moves slowly, yet His grace comes.

———— * ————

The person not taught by God is not taught by man.

———— * ————

What God sends is far away.

———— * ————

God shares the good things.

———— * ————

God never closes one door without opening another.

The love of God guides every good.

———— * ————

Whatever God has given me, I cannot sell.

———— * ————

Man talks but God directs.

———— * ————

The grace of God is between the saddle and the ground.

———— * ————

God is good, but the devil is not so bad either.

CHURCH

Those who go to church are not all saints.

———— * ————

A big church yields small devotions.

———— * ————

The nearer the church, the further from God.

———— * ————

Be neither intimate nor distant with the clergy.

———— * ————

The priest's pig gets the most porridge.

———— * ————

A dumb priest never got a parish.

———— * ————

Put the priest in the middle of the parish.

———— * ————

Although there was nobody present but the priest and the friar, still I have lost all my property.

———— * ————

Don't be mean and don't be generous with the clergy.

———— * ————

A good sweep of the kitchen is as good as a prayer in the chapel.

It's his own child the priest baptizes first.

———— * ————

The way of the nuns with the country women—they receive a great lump and give a small return.

———— * ————

A priest that's made a pet of and a pig that's made a pet of are the two worst pets of all.

———— * ————

If there's a hen or a goose it's surely on the priest's table it will be.

THE DEVIL

The devil waits his day.

———— * ————

It's easy to preach to the devil with a full stomach.

———— * ————

Never bid the devil good morrow until you meet him.

———— * ————

Speak to the devil and you'll hear the thunder of his hooves.

———— * ————

The man of horns is active.

———— * ————

Needs must when the devil rides.

———— * ————

To praise God is proper, but a wise man won't blackguard the devil.

———— * ————

The devil never took a good heart to hell.

———— * ————

Better is the devil you know than the devil you don't know.

———— * ————

You may as well go to hell with a load as with a *pahil*.

[A *pahil* is a small bundle.]

———— * ————

The devil always leaves a stink behind him.

———— * ————

The devil dances in an empty pocket.

———— * ————

The devil wipes his tail with the poor man's pride.

———— * ————

Let one devil beat another.

———— * ————

The devil loves no holy water.

———— * ————

The devil is busy in a gale of wind.

———— * ————

The devil is kind to his own.

———— * ————

The devil is a busy bishop in his own diocese.

———— * ————

Hell is always open.

MATTERS OF LIFE
AND DEATH

D. Maclise, R.A.

F. P. Becker.

LIFE

We live as long as we're let.

———— * ————

Life lies not in living, but in liking.

———— * ————

Twenty years agrowing, twenty years at rest, twenty years
declining, and twenty years when it doesn't matter whether
you're there or not.

———— * ————

We live in one another's shadows.

———— * ————

You will live during the year for we were just talking of
you.

———— * ————

You must take the little potato with the big potato.

YOUTH AND AGE

Young people don't know what age is, and old people
forget what youth was.

———— * ————

It's difficult to put an old head on a young shoulder.

———— * ————

Bend the sapling while it is young.

———— * ————

Praise the young and they will make progress.

———— * ————

Youth likes to wander.

———— * ————

Make your hay before the fine weather leaves you.

———— * ————

Youth often sheds its skin.

———— * ————

Old age is a heavy burden.

———— * ————

To be old and decayed dishonors no one.

———— * ————

Honor belongs to old age.

———— * ————

When the twig hardens, it is difficult to twist it.

———— * ————

It is not a lonesome thing to be getting old.

———— * ————

Good sense comes only with age.

———— * ————

In youth we have our troubles before us; in age we leave
pleasure behind.

———— * ————

The old man hasn't the place of the cat in the ashes.

———— * ————

The older the fiddle, the sweeter the tune.

HEALTH

A healthy man is king.

———— * ————

Health is better than flocks.

———— * ————

Health is better than wealth.

———— * ————

The herb that can't be got is the one that brings relief.

———— * ————

The medicine that hurts the most is generally the best healer.

———— * ————

A good laugh and a long sleep are the best cures in a doctor's book.

———— * ————

He who cannot suffer pain will not get ease.

———— * ————

A good diet cures better than the doctor.

———— * ————

It's better to pay the cook than the doctor.

———— * ————

Sickness is the physician's feast.

———— * ————

May we be preserved from lawyers and from doctors.

———— * ————

The beginning of a ship is a board, of a kiln a stone, of a king's reign salutation, and the beginning of health is sleep.

———— * ————

A sick man said to be dead always recovers.

———— * ————

Troubles come one by one; health will come by force of will.

———— * ————

A long disease doesn't tell a lie; it kills at last.

———— * ————

Bones will gather flesh while the marrow is sound.

———— * ————

The relapse is worse than the final fever.

———— * ————

Every patient is a doctor after his own cure.

———— * ————

He who is dying every day will live the longest.

———— * ————

What butter or whiskey will not cure there's no cure for.

———— * ————

Whiskey when you're sick makes you well; whiskey when you're well makes you sick.

———— * ————

The person who doesn't scatter the morning dew will not comb gray hairs.

———— * ————

It's unbecoming for a carpenter to be heavy-handed, a smith to be shaky-handed, or a physician to be tender-hearted.

———— * ————

Sickness begins with a cough and ends with a coffin.

———— * ————

Patience is the cure for an old illness.

———— * ————

The physician's hope — every misfortune.

———— * ————

One must pay health its tithes.

———— * ————

What cannot be cured must be endured.

DEATH

Physicians disagree and patients die.

Many a day we shall rest in the clay.

———— * ————

May God spare anyone who has a hand in his own death.

———— * ————

Death stares the old in the face and lurks behind the backs of the young.

———— * ————

Don't run for the priest *after* the patient has died.

———— * ————

There is many a person with a high head today who will be lying low tomorrow.

———— * ————

There is no man's death without another man's gain.

———— * ————

You'll be going yet and your two feet before you.

———— * ————

Death never comes too late.

———— * ————

Death does not take a bribe.

———— * ————

It is not the tree that is a long time shaking that is the first to fall.

———— * ————

Opening a grave has frequently been another man's opening to possessions.

———— * ————

The oldest man that ever lived died at last.

———— * ————

Any death is easier than death by the sword.

———— * ————

Death is the poor man's best physician.

———— * ————

There is hope from the mouth of the sea but none from the mouth of the grave.

———— * ————

There's neither herb nor cure for death.

———— * ————

Death does not come without a cause.

———— * ————

Sleep is the brother of death.

———— * ————

Deathbed repentence is like sowing seed at Martinmas.

[Martinmas is in the cold month of November!]

———— * ————

The trace of the hand will live, but not the hand that made it.

———— * ————

Death and flitting are hard on housekeeping.

[Flitting = changing residence (also a metaphor for dying)]

———— * ————

To die and to lose one's life are much the same thing.

———— * ————

The last sigh will be painful.

RICH AND POOR
FRIEND AND NEIGHBOR

D.Maclise, R.A.

T.Landseer.

Rich and Poor

Sweet is the voice of the man who has wealth.

———— * ————

Neither sea nor mountain can deprive a prosperous man of his possessions, but the unfortunate man cannot retain a rivulet.

———— * ————

A shamefaced man seldom acquires wealth.

———— * ————

The doorstep of a great house is slippery.

———— * ————

A heavy purse makes a light heart.

———— * ————

The more you get, the less you have.

———— * ————

Better be bordering on plenty than be in the very middle of poverty.

———— * ————

It's easy to knead when meal is at hand.

———— * ————

Though you love your wealth, keep your good name, for if you lose that, you are worthless.

———— * ————

The man whose stomach is well-filled does not understand the needs of the hungry.

———— * ————

Better own a trifle than want a great deal.

———— * ————

Without money fame is dead.

———— * ————

The moneymaker is never tired.

———— * ————

Misfortune comes only where wealth is.

———— * ————

Your pocket is your friend.

———— * ————

There is no tune without a penny.

———— * ————

Poverty parts good company.

———— * ————

A poor man never yet lost his property.

———— * ————

Poverty is no shame, but shame is ever a part of poverty.

———— * ————

The poor are pleased with buttermilk.

———— * ————

Many a defect is seen in the poor man.

———— * ————

The thief is no danger to the beggar.

———— * ————

It's hard to take britches off bare hips.

———— * ————

There is nothing in the world so poor as going to hell.

———— * ————

The luxurious poor will not be rich.

———— * ————

Pity the man who does wrong and is poor as well.

———— * ————

A poor fellow can do but his best.

———— * ————

There is no need for the poor's wisdom, nor for a palace in the wilderness.

———— * ————

It's no use carrying an umbrella if your shoes are leaking.

———— * ————

A poor man is pleased with whatever he gets.

———— * ————

The law of borrowing is to break the borrower.

———— * ————

If you must be in rags, let your rags be tidy.

———— * ————

Those who have not meat find soup a luxury.

———— * ————

A penny in a poor man's pocket is better than two pennies in a rich man's pocket.

———— * ————

No one is ever poor who has the sight of his eyes and the use of his feet.

———— * ————

Though high above the poor the rich may look, they will be all together yet.

FRIENDS AND NEIGHBORS

Prove a friend before you need him.

———— * ————

Tell me who your friends are and I'll tell you who you are.

———— * ————

Friendship will not stand on one leg.

Friends are better than gold.

———— * ————

Take care but take no sides and on no account sacrifice your friends.

———— * ————

Friendship conceals blemishes.

———— * ————

Pick your company before you sit down.

———— * ————

A friend in court is better than a coin in the pocket.

———— * ————

The friend that can be bought is not worth buying.

———— * ————

Friendship is good though separation is painful.

———— * ————

Reckoning up is friendship's end.

———— * ————

A constant guest is never welcome.

———— * ————

Reverence ceases once blood is spilled.

———— * ————

Don't show your skin to the person who won't cover it.

———— * ————

The coldness of a friend, like the coldness of linen, never lasts long.

———— * ————

Two persons never lit a fire without disagreeing.

———— * ————

Better a little of one's own than many friends.

———— * ————

Quarreling among relatives and peace among enemies— two things that need not be considered.

———— * ————

He who holds his tongue keeps his friend.

———— * ————

The coldness of a friend is better than the sweetness of an enemy.

———— * ————

If you will walk with lame men you will soon limp yourself.

———— * ————

It is better to be alone than in bad company.

———— * ————

The man long absent is forgotten.

———— * ————

Be mild with the wretched but stern with your enemy.

———— * ————

A friend's eye is a good looking glass.

———— * ————

A little help is better than a lot of pity.

———— * ————

When the hand ceases to scatter, the mouth ceases to praise.

———— * ————

Take a gift with a sigh; most men give to be paid.

———— * ————

Don't put your friend in your pocket.

———— * ————

A friend's advice, unasked, is never appreciated as it ought to be.

———— * ————

Bare is one's back unless he have a brother.

———— * ————

Two are stronger together, than far apart, in crossing a stream.

———— * ————

Better an ounce of blood than a pound of friendship.

— * —

Faithful are the wounds of a friend, but an enemy's kisses
are deceitful.

— * —

Woe to him who gives his neighbor a choice.

— * —

There is more friendship in a jigger of whiskey than in a
churn of buttermilk.

— * —

Pity the man in a country where there is none to take his
part.

— * —

Kick him again—he's not family.

— * —

Bad as I like ye, it's worse without ye.

— * —

WISE MAN AND FOOL

F. P. Becker.

Wise Man and Fool

There are two things that can't be cured — death and
stupidity.

———— * ————

Everyone is wise until he speaks.

———— * ————

Though wisdom is good in the beginning, it is better at the
end.

———— * ————

A wise man will form a year's judgment from one night's
knowledge of another man.

———— * ————

A wise head keeps a shut mouth.

———— * ————

A little of anything isn't worth a bean, but a little bit of
sense is worth a lot.

———— * ————

There's no making a man wise.

———— * ————

He may die of wind, but he'll never die of wisdom.

———— * ————

The wise man's opinion comes nearest the truth.

———— * ————

Wisdom is what makes a poor man a king, a weak person powerful, a good generation of a bad one, and a foolish man reasonable.

———— * ————

There's never been a wise man without a fault.

———— * ————

The person with least knowledge talks most.

———— * ————

Food is no more important than wisdom.

———— * ————

Better knowledge of evil than evil without knowledge.

———— * ————

There will not be one wise man among a thousand fools.

———— * ————

The *amadán* fell into the fire and the *óinseach* began to cry.

[In Irish an *amadán* is a male fool and an *óinseach* a female fool.]

———— * ————

The *óinseach* sees the *amadán*'s faults.

———— * ————

The fool may pass for wise if he holds his tongue.

———— * ————

The fool has luck.

———— * ————

Anger may look in on a wise man's heart, but it abides in the heart of a fool.

———— * ————

Often a fool's son is a wise man.

———— * ————

Crafty advice is often got from a fool.

———— * ————

Don't give cherries to pigs; don't give advice to fools.

———— * ————

A fool's word is like a thorn concealed in mud.

[That is, it stings one unexpectedly.]

———— * ————

No fools are so intolerable as those who affect to be wits.

———— * ————

When fools make mistakes they lay the blame on
Providence.

———— * ————

More know Tom the Fool than Tom the Fool knows.

———— * ————

Gold is light with a fool.

———— * ————

Sweet words beguile a fool.

———— * ————

It's a trifle that makes fools laugh.

———— * ————

A big head on a wise man and a hen's head on a fool.

———— * ————

Give me that and be a fool yourself.

[An offhand dismissal of a request thought unreasonable.]

———— * ————

He's a fool who'll not take advice, but he's a thousand
times worse who takes every advice.

———— * ————

Give a clown his choice and he'll choose the worst.

———— * ————

Counsel fit for a king often comes from a fool.

———— * ————

He who has the thickest skull has the smallest brain.

LUCK AND
MISFORTUNE

D. Machse, R.A.   F.P. Becker

LUCK AND MISFORTUNE

Good luck comes in slender currents; misfortune comes in
rolling torrents.

——— * ———

It's better to be lucky than rich.

——— * ———

Good luck is better than early rising.

——— * ———

Fortune is a good thing, but it's worth searching for it.

——— * ———

No door closes without opening another door.

——— * ———

Luck seldom lasts.

——— * ———

The ugly are often lucky and the handsome unfortunate.

——— * ———

A chance shot will not kill the devil.

——— * ———

One hapless act may undo a man, and one timely one will
reestablish him.

——— * ———

The man who has luck in the morning has luck in the
afternoon.

Luck's a king and luck's a beggar.

———— * ————

There is luck in sharing.

———— * ————

Whose word is not his bond, his luck will never stand.

———— * ————

It's better to be lucky than wise.

———— * ————

A fool has all the luck.

———— * ————

A meeting in the sunlight is lucky, and a burying in the rain.

———— * ————

There is no luck unless there is authority.

———— * ————

The fortunate man waits for prosperity, and the unfortunate takes a leap in the dark.

———— * ————

The lucky person has only to be born.

———— * ————

Misfortunes never come singly.

———— * ————

When luck comes it comes by the bucketload.

———— * ————

Prosperity often comes to the easygoing.

———— * ————

Often does the likely fail and the unlikely prosper.

———— * ————

There is no heightening the grief of a sorrowful man.

———— * ————

The old white horse is the end of all misfortune.

———— * ————

A man sleeps very soundly on another man's hurt.

———— * ————

Speak to misfortune when it comes.

———— * ————

We go from the house of the devil to the house of the demon.

———— * ————

Nothing is ever as bad as it seems.

———— * ————

After misfortune the Irishman sees his profit.

———— * ————

There's worse than this in the North.

———— * ————

Waves will rise on silent water.

———— * ————

It is well that misfortunes come one by one and not all together.

———— * ————

He who is in straits must make a shift some way.

———— * ————

Exigencies come to kings.

———— * ————

When misfortune is greatest, relief is nearest.

———— * ————

Let each person judge his own luck, good or bad.

91

TOIL AND LABOR

Toil and Labor

The sweat of one's brow is what burns everyone.

———— * ————

If he's not fishing, he's mending his nets.

[Said of an enterprising man who plans ahead.]

———— * ————

Making the beginning is one-third of the work.

———— * ————

The early riser gets through his business but not through early rising.

———— * ————

There's no need to fear the wind if your haystacks are tied down.

———— * ————

The seeking for one thing will find another.

———— * ————

If the knitter is weary, the baby will have no new bonnet.

———— * ————

Do it as if there were fire in your skin.

———— * ————

A farmer's work is never done.

———— * ————

You'll never plow a field by turning it over in your mind.

What is well done will be shown by results.

———— * ————

A man may force a livelihood, but he cannot force fortune.

———— * ————

Better not to begin than to stop without finishing.

———— * ————

The man who waits for a good day will get it.

———— * ————

Early sow, early mow.

———— * ————

Lazy is lazy in going to bed, but seven times lazier to rise.

———— * ————

Don't go early or late to the well.

———— * ————

Night is a good shepherd: it brings home man and beast.

———— * ————

Handfuls make a load.

———— * ————

If it's you that's needed, let the labor be yours.

———— * ————

The dog that's always on the go is better than the one that's always curled up.

———— * ————

One day in March is better than three days in autumn.
[One good spring day's work will give more than three days' harvesting.]

———— * ————

It destroys the craft not to learn it.

———— * ————

He who does his work in time will always have leisure time.

———— * ————

He who will not sow on a cold day will not reap on a warm day.

The mason who strikes often is better than the one who strikes too hard.

———— * ————

He who does not work the small farm is unworthy of a big one.

———— * ————

It's no delay to stop to edge the scythe.

———— * ————

He who will not tie a knot will lose his first stitch.

———— * ————

A little man can take his share from the land when a tall man cannot take his from the sky.

———— * ————

Put it on your shoulder and say it is not a burden.

———— * ————

Industry pays debts.

———— * ————

Scattering is easier than gathering.

———— * ————

The industrious lad's morsel is on every dish.

———— * ————

Feeding the land before it gets hungry, giving it rest before it gets weary, and weeding it well before it gets dirty are the marks of a good husbandman.

———— * ————

Two never prospered on the same hill.

———— * ————

Long churning makes bad butter.

———— * ————

A late beginning will not mend a bad day's work.

———— * ————

Better a handful of craftsmanship than a handful of gold.

Be there with the day and be gone with the day.

———— * ————

Better the diligence of the weak man than the indifference
of a strong man.

———— * ————

The person of the greatest talk is the person of the least
work.

———— * ————

Better small corn seeds out of bad land than no seed at all.

———— * ————

Fat is not to be had without labor.

———— * ————

I'll go there tonight for evening is speedier than morning.

———— * ————

Better be idle than working for nothing.

———— * ————

You thought to reap wheat where you sowed nothing but
hemlock.

———— * ————

Speed and accuracy do not agree.

———— * ————

Long sleep makes a bare back.

———— * ————

Many a little makes a mickle.

———— * ————

Winter comes fast on the lazy.

———— * ————

The speckled-shins of spring is the envious one of autumn.
[One gets speckled shins by lounging near the fire.]

———— * ————

As you have spent the candle, spend the inch.
[As you have gone most of the way, go the whole way.]

TRIADS

TRIADS

Three things that are not to be trusted—a fine day in winter, the life of an aged person, and the word of a man of importance unless it is in writing.

———— * ————

Three things that cannot be acquired—a voice, generosity, and poetry.

———— * ————

The three most difficult things to touch—a woman, a pig, and a mule.

———— * ————

Three things that are never seen—a blade's edge, wind, and love.

———— * ————

Three kinds of poor people—the man who is poor by force of circumstance, the man who is poor voluntarily, and the man who is poor even though he owns the world (i.e., the miser).

———— * ————

Three signs of an unfortunate man—going bail, intervening in disputes and bearing testimony.

———— * ————

Three acts of kindness that are unrequited—that done for

an old man, for a wicked person, or for a little child.

———— * ————

Three things that are as good as their betters—a wooden sword in a coward's hand, an ugly wife married to a blind man, and ragged clothes on a drunkard.

———— * ————

The three things most difficult to go through—a waterfall, a bog, and a briary path.

———— * ————

The three most vexing things—a thorn in the foot, and a woman and a goat going to the fair who will go any way but the way you want them to.

———— * ————

Three things that are of little use—a button and no buttonhole, a trumpet and no tongue, and a wolf without teeth.

———— * ————

The three worst things to have in a house—a shrewish wife, a smoky chimney, and a leaky roof.

———— * ————

Three things that are futile—throwing a stone on a bend, giving advice to an angry woman, and talking to a head without sense.

———— * ————

Three things a man should not be without—a cat, a chimney, and a wife.

———— * ————

Three parts of the body most easily hurt—the knee, the elbow, and the eye.

———— * ————

The three happiest creatures in the world—the tailor, the piper, and the goat.

———— * ————

The three sweetest melodies—the churning of butter, the plow plowing, and the mill grinding.

———— * ————

The three best friends that are also the three worst enemies—fire, wind, and rain.

———— * ————

Three signs of the unlucky man—long visits to his neighbors, long morning sleep, and bad fences.

———— * ————

Three signs of the lucky man—diligence, early rising, and good fences.

———— * ————

The three most difficult things to choose—a wife, a scythe, and a razor.

———— * ————

The three worst flittings—leaving mass before it ends, leaving table without grace, and leaving your wife to go to another woman.

———— * ————

Three things that arrive unnoticed—rent, age, and a beard.

———— * ————

Three things that stay longest in a family—fighting, thieving, and red hair.

———— * ————

Three creatures that do not clean their snouts—the dog, the pig, and the farmer.

———— * ————

Three traits of the drunkard—a wretched morning, a dirty coat, and empty pockets.

———— * ————

Three essential truths—sunrise, sunset, and death.

———— * ————

Three things that are best when small—a beehive, a sheep, and a woman.

———— * ————

Three things to have in abundance—sunshine, wisdom, and generosity.

———— * ————

Three kinds of men who rise early—the husband of a jabbering wife, the man with a stolen white horse, and the man with a ragged dirty shirt.

———— * ————

The three loveliest sights to see—a garden of white potatoes in blossom, a ship under sail, and a wife after giving birth.

———— * ————

The three worst endings—a house burning, a ship sinking, and an old white horse dying.

———— * ————

Three things that relate to drink—to carry it, to pay for it, and to consume it.

———— * ————

The three coldest things in the world—a dog's snout, a man's knee, and a woman's breast.

———— * ————

Three oaths that money swore—that it did not care who would possess it, that it would stay but a while with any man, and that it would not stay with any man save the man who loved it.

———— * ————

Three pairs that never agree—two married women in the same house, two cats with one mouse, and two bachelors courting the same young woman.

———— * ————

The three strongest forces—the force of fire, the force of water, and the force of hatred.

———— * ————

Three things that are as good as the best—dirty water to quench a fire, a frieze coat on a wintry day, and black bread in the time of famine.

———— * ————

Three kinds of brains—brains as hard as stone, brains as receptive as wax, and brains as unstable as flowing water.

———— * ————

The three most nourishing foods—beef marrow, the meat of a chicken, and Irish stout.

———— * ————

The three worst pets—a pet priest, a pet beggar, and a pet pig.

———— * ————

Three good things to have—a clean shirt, a clean conscience, and a guinea in the pocket.

———— * ————

Three things that won't have rest—a steep waterfall, an otter, and a devil out of hell.

———— * ————

Three men the devil can take without much trouble—the mason, the bailiff, and the miller.

———— * ————

Three great evils—smallness of house, closeness of heart, and shortage of food.

———— * ————

Three places that can't be avoided—the place of birth, the place of death, and the place of burial.

———— * ————

The three greatest rushes—the rush of water, the rush of

fire, and the rush of falsehood.

——— * ———

Three enemies of the body—wind, smoke, and fleas.

——— * ———

Three bad habits—drinking the pint, smoking the pipe, and scattering the dew late at night.

——— * ———

The three best invitations—come to mass, come and make secure, and come to the mill.

——— * ———

Three things that can never return—a day away from school, a Sunday without mass, and a day away from one's trade.

——— * ———

Three things that are useless when old—an old schoolmaster, an old horse, and an old soldier.

——— * ———

Three things that are not to be trusted—a hound's tooth, a horse's hoof, and a gentleman's word.

——— * ———

Three kinds of men—the worker, the pleasure-seeker, and the boaster.

——— * ———

Three places to be avoided—a doctor's door, a priest's door, and a barracks door.

WORDS
TO THE WISE

Words to the Wise

Humor is like a feather pillow—it is filled with what is easy to get, but gives great comfort.

———— * ————

A blind man can see his mouth.

———— * ————

Watching is part of a good play.

———— * ————

It's hard to fight with the wide ocean.

———— * ————

A short visit is best, and that of short duration.

———— * ————

An Irishman before answering a question always asks another.

———— * ————

The stars make no noise.

———— * ————

To address a head without knowledge is like the barking of a dog in a green valley.

———— * ————

"Will you" was never a good fellow.

———— * ————

If you give away an old coat, don't cut off the buttons.

The man who was dividing Ireland didn't leave himself last.

———— * ————

It wasn't on one leg St. Patrick came to Ireland.

———— * ————

White collars sometimes hide dirty necks.

———— * ————

Don't kick till you're spurred.

———— * ————

A word goes to the winds, but a blow goes to the bones.

———— * ————

The best way to keep loyalty in a man's heart is to keep money in his pocket.

———— * ————

Every foot is slow on an unknown path.

———— * ————

When angry words arise, a closed mouth is soothing.

———— * ————

When the sky falls, we'll all catch larks.

———— * ————

To be redheaded is better than to be without a head.

———— * ————

Don't see all you see, and don't hear all you hear.

———— * ————

Beauty does not make the pot boil.

———— * ————

An Irishman is never at peace except when he's fighting.

———— * ————

A big belly was never generous.

———— * ————

A sweet tongue is rarely without a sting to it.

———— * ————

It's better to be sorry and stay than be sorry and go away.

Long as the day may be, the night comes at last.

———— * ————

A silent mouth is musical.

———— * ————

The good that is is better than the good that was.

———— * ————

Any man can lose his hat in a fairy-wind.

———— * ————

There's always one more son of a bitch than you counted on.

———— * ————

None knows where the shoe pinches better than the wearer.

———— * ————

One pair of good soles is worth two pairs of uppers.

———— * ————

An Irish game has an Irish trick or vengeance.

———— * ————

The thing that's not eaten and not stolen will be found.

———— * ————

The longest road out is the shortest road home.

———— * ————

A patch is better than a hole, but a hole is more honorable than a patch.

———— * ————

Keep your tongue in your jaw and your toe in your shoe.

———— * ————

Rear to the wind and front to the sun's heat.

———— * ————

Irish roads are potholes loosely joined together with tarmac.

———— * ————

A scholar's ink lasts longer than a martyr's blood.

———— * ————

Never pour water on a drowned mouse.

———— * ————

You won't make a rope from the sand of the sea.

———— * ————

Hope soothes the tired heart.

———— * ————

Too much of one thing is the same as nothing.

———— * ————

Irish sexual compatability is when a husband and his wife both have headaches on the same night.

———— * ————

Do not be breaking a shin on a stool that's not in your way.

———— * ————

Soft words butter no parsnips, but they won't harden the heart of a cabbage either.

———— * ————

A story without an author is not worth listening to.

———— * ————

A lie looks the better of having a witness.

———— * ————

Do not keep your tongue under your belt.

———— * ————

A foot at rest meets nothing.

———— * ————

By degrees the castles are built.

———— * ————

He who is born under a three-penny planet will never be worth a groat.

———— * ————

The Irish forgive their great men when they are safely buried.

———— * ————

A man may be his own ruin; a wedge from itself splits the oak tree.

———— * ————

A poem ought to be well made at first, for there is many a one to ruin it afterwards.

———— * ————

The only time England can use an Irishman is when he emigrates to America and votes for Free Trade.

———— * ————

Get an Irishman on the spit and you'll easily find two others to turn him.

———— * ————

Never run after a bus or a woman. There will always be another one along in a few minutes.

———— * ————

When it is raining porridge the beggars have no spoons.

———— * ————

Face the sun but turn your back to the storm.

———— * ————

The Leinster man is sprightly, the Munster man boastful, the Connaught man sweet-tongued, and the Ulster man impudent.

———— * ————

An Irishman carries his heart in his hand.

———— * ————

It's a very good time if it lasts.

———— * ————

He that's born to be hanged needn't fear water.

———— * ————

Cleaning the house will not pay the rent.

———— * ————

Beware of the hoof of the horse, the horn of the bull, and

the smile of the Englishman.

———— * ————

Where an Irishman can enjoy a potato patch and a cow he is happy enough.

———— * ————

The one who loses the game has the liberty of talking.

———— * ————

Without provisions, no friends; without rearing, no manners.

———— * ————

Snuff at a wake is fine—if there's nobody sneezing over the snuffbox.

———— * ————

It isn't a man's clothes that tell how much he earns, but his wife's.

———— * ————

Better come at the end of a fast than the beginning of a quarrel.

———— * ————

Never put out your hand farther than you can draw it back again.

———— * ————

It's no secret that's known to three.

———— * ————

The best thing that could happen to England would be for Ireland to be submerged in the Atlantic for twenty-four hours.

———— * ————

Do not take the thatch from your own house to buy slates for another man's roof.

———— * ————

A secret is a weapon and a friend.

———— * ————

A sword, a spade, and a thought should never be allowed to rust.

———— * ————

White collars sometimes hide dirty necks.

———— * ————

Nature passes nurture.

———— * ————

Say but little and say it well.

———— * ————

Trampling on dung only spreads it the more.

———— * ————

Praise the sea but stay close to land.

———— * ————

Better a son who gambles than a son who drinks.

———— * ————

A kind word never broke anyone's mouth.

———— * ————

To know a person one must live in the same house with him.

———— * ————

Don't throw out the dirty water until you have the clean.

———— * ————

Do not show your teeth until you can bite.

———— * ————

The hope of winning is what beggars the gambler.

———— * ————

Though there is no bone in the tongue, it has often broken a person's head.

———— * ————

If it's worth taking, it's worth asking for.

———— * ————

What is got by guile will disappear with the wind.

———— * ————

The little frequent will overtake the infrequent large.

———— * ————

Money is like manure, no good until you spread it around.

———— * ————

You will never know a man until you do business with him.

———— * ————

There is no deceit as great as a promise unfulfilled.

———— * ————

The deaf will hear the clink of money.

———— * ————

The coxcomb feels no cold no matter how cold the day.

———— * ————

A good tale is not the worse of being twice told.

———— * ————

There is no such thing as a hero without compare.

———— * ————

The thief has only two eyes, but there are a dozen eyes watching him.

———— * ————

Despise your old shoes when you get new ones.

———— * ————

Though the silk be fine, it cares not who wears it.

———— * ————

Hesitation in buying is better than delay in paying.

———— * ————

Wear is better than rust.

———— * ————

The upright heart endures a great deal before it breaks.

———— * ————

Empty bladders are loquacious.

———— * ————

An empty pail makes most noise.

———— * ————

Justice melts in the mouths of the faint-hearted.

———— * ————

If you have only one eye, look with the eye you've got.

———— * ————

Do not light a fire you cannot yourself put out.

———— * ————

Do not pluck the beard of a stranger.

———— * ————

Put silk on a stick and it will look fine.

———— * ————

The Irishman's wit is on his tongue.

———— * ————

The waves have some mercy, but the rocks have no mercy at all.

———— * ————

You can protect yourself from a thief, but not from a liar.

———— * ————

The world will pass away, but love and music last for aye.

———— * ————

The diligent weak will beat the lazy strong.

———— * ————

He who speaks the lowest hears the best.

———— * ————

It is afterwards events are understood.

———— * ————

He who is quickest to promise is also the quickest to deceive.

———— * ————

A blow that is not struck is not actionable at law.

———— * ————

He who has not learned at the knee will not learn at the elbow.

———— * ————

A fool's tongue is long enough to cut his own throat.

———— * ————

He who is late in rising will be in a hurry all day.

———— * ————

He who will not listen to father or mother will listen to what will please him less—the calf's skin.

[i.e., a leather strap.]

———— * ————

A person is often a bad adviser to himself and a good adviser to another.

———— * ————

He who will not listen to what he does not like will not see what will please him.

———— * ————

There is no vanity in the dress, but in the one who buys it.

———— * ————

A man's tongue will often give him a big bite to chew.

———— * ————

Do not boast of your father or of your mother, but prove by your own conduct that you are a gentleman.

———— * ————

Better a good deed which is boasted of than no good deed at all.

———— * ————

Better one good thing that is than two good things that were.

———— * ————

Better "it is so" than "it may be so."

———— * ————

Forgetting a debt does not pay it.

———— * ————

Avoid the person who considers his opinion a certainty.

———— * ————

Be afraid and you'll be safe.

———— * ————

Go to a man who is in difficulty and you'll get a bargain.

———— * ————

The youngest thorn is the sharpest.

———— * ————

The Irishman is an impatient fellow.

———— * ————

Don't blow on dead embers.

———— * ————

Coming out is a different thing from going in.

———— * ————

Mere words will not feed the friars.

———— * ————

Limerick was, Dublin is, and Cork will be the most
important city in Ireland.

———— * ————

An inch is a great deal in a man's nose.

———— * ————

After a gathering comes a scattering.

———— * ————

Time and patience would bring a snail to America.

———— * ————

A good run is better than a bad stand.

———— * ————

A buckle is a great addition to an old shoe.

———— * ————

Sex is the only game that becomes less exciting when
played for money.

———— * ————

"Turnabout is fair play," as the devil said to the smokejack.

———— * ————

He that spies is the one that kills.

A sly rogue is often well-dressed.

———— * ————

You must empty a box before you fill it again.

———— * ————

A vessel will only hold its contents.

———— * ————

The covetous man is always in want.

———— * ————

It's a good story that fills the belly.

———— * ————

Many a sudden change takes place in a spring day.

———— * ————

There's anger in an open laugh.

———— * ————

A spender gets the property of the hoarder.

———— * ————

About evening a man is known.

———— * ————

It's the empty car that makes the most noise.

———— * ————

Black stones will never grow white.

———— * ————

Hills that are far away look green.

———— * ————

A man with a loud laugh makes truth itself seem foolish.

———— * ————

Let the tail go with the hide.

———— * ————

It's no joke going to law with the devil, and the court held in hell.

———— * ————

Even contention is better than loneliness.

———— * ————

Hope is the physician of each misery.

———— * ————

Better April showers than the breadth of the ocean in gold.

———— * ————

A spur in the head is worth two in the heel.

———— * ————

Fear is a fine spur; so is rage.

———— * ————

Great minds live apart; people may meet, but mountains and rocks never.

———— * ————

It is difficult to soothe the proud.

———— * ————

Don't say everything you like lest you hear a thing you would not like.

———— * ————

Look at the river before you cross the ferry.

———— * ————

The heaviest ear of corn is the one that bends its head the lowest.

———— * ————

If you buy a bad thing, you will soon buy again.

———— * ————

Falling is easier than rising.

———— * ————

Falsehood often goes further than truth.

———— * ————

The mother of mischief is no bigger than a midge's wing.

———— * ————

A good retreat is better than a poor defence.

———— * ————

What I am afraid may be said to me I had better say first myself.

Fences have ears.

———— * ————

Praise the ripe field, not the green corn.

———— * ————

To think of it is as good as to mention it.

———— * ————

No matter who comes off well, the peacemaker is sure to come off ill.

———— * ————

Fame is longer than life.

———— * ————

A look before is better than two behind.

———— * ————

Proverbs cannot be contradicted.

———— * ————

Bribery can split a stone.

———— * ————

Row with the oar that's nearest at hand.

———— * ————

The more you get of what's good, the less you'll get of what's bad.

———— * ————

What is delayed will be forgotten.

———— * ————

A man's faults will be as large as a mountain before he sees them.

———— * ————

Desperation will give courage to a coward.

———— * ————

There is no profit without loss.

———— * ————

A curse breaks no bones.

———— * ————

A blessing feeds no one.

———— * ————

Promising but not fulfilling is worse than refusing.

———— * ————

A shaken trust is worse than no trust at all.

———— * ————

A small spark has often kindled a great fire.

———— * ————

A rich heart may be under a poor coat.

———— * ————

He who speaks of all he sees will hear what will shame him.

———— * ————

He who will not flee will be fled from.

———— * ————

Housekeeping is not possible on empty shelves.

———— * ————

The end of the day is no less in God's sight than the beginning.

———— * ————

It's only good to be hungry when you have something to eat.

———— * ————

The best apple will be on the highest bough.

———— * ————

Quick to love, quick to hate.

———— * ————

A promise can never be tethered.

———— * ————

Where the river is shallowest, it will make the most noise.

———— * ————

The first served is never hungry.

———— * ————

Any color will take black, but black will not take any color.

———— * ————

Save a coin and spend a coin, and you'll be happy.

———— * ————

Save a coin and spend one not, unhappiness will be your lot.

———— * ————

Bribe the rogue and you needn't fear the honest man.

———— * ————

Cattle are caught by their horns, people by their tongues.

———— * ————

Put mouth to mouth, but not pen to paper.

———— * ————

A change of job is as good as a vacation.

———— * ————

The good deed boasted of is little; the good deed unacknowledged is little better.

———— * ————

If the bare part of the hill is bad, the summit is worse.

———— * ————

A sting often lurks behind a kiss.

———— * ————

Often there is great darkness with little rain.

———— * ————

A crooked cane makes a straight back.

———— * ————

If you stretch out with your hand, you will reach out with your feet.

———— * ————

A small stain will ruin white stockings.

———— * ————

The river is no wider from one side than the other.

———— * ————

It's a wise thing to always have some story on the tip of your tongue.

———— * ————

Woe to the man drowned in a storm, for after the rain comes the sunshine.

———— * ————

What kills one man gives life to another.

———— * ————

An empty sack can't stand.

———— * ————

Only God can make a race horse out of a jackass.

———— * ————

There is no cure for grief but to put it underfoot.

———— * ————

There's no happiness without an inch of sorrow.

———— * ————

Both night and day are as long as they ever were.

———— * ————

Crying is not far away from laughter.

———— * ————

One liar knows another.

———— * ————

Neither break a law nor make one.

———— * ————

The hand goes only where the leg goes.

———— * ————

When the apple is ripe, it will fall.

———— * ————

Don't tell your troubles to someone who has no pity.

———— * ————

A man has often cut a rod to beat himself.

———— * ————

Silence is the same as confession.

———— * ————

A man's mouth can break his nose.

———— * ————

A good name is easier lost than gained.

———— * ————

The upright is upright from head to foot.

———— * ————

A turf fire and a boy's love never last long.

———— * ————

The weed that grows from the dunghill lifts its head the highest.

———— * ————

The grass that grows in March will shrink away in April.

———— * ————

Just as far as the wind enters through the door on St. Brigid's Day, so far will the snowdrift enter on St. Patrick's Day.

[St. Brigid's Day is February Ist.]

———— * ————

Pity the man who entrusts his secrets to a ditch.

———— * ————

Kerry security—bond, pledge, oath, and keep the money.

———— * ————

A dark man is bold; a fair man, officious; a brown man, tortuous; and a red man scornful.

———— * ————

Any man can laugh on a hillside.

———— * ————

Every creature will suffer being good except the son of man.

———— * ————

Index

Age, 67-68
Animals, 15–35
Ants, 34
Asses, 15

Badgers, 15
Bees, 34
Beetles, 34
Birds, 29-33
Bulls, 15

Calves, 16
Cats, 16-18
Chickens, 30-31
Children, 46-48
Church, 62-63
Cows, 18-19
Crows, 31

Death, 70-71
Deer, 19-20
Devil, 63-64
Dogs, 20-22
Donkeys, 23
Doves, 31
Drink, 55-57
Ducks, 31

Fish, 33-34
Flies, 34-35
Food, 52-55
Foolishness, 83-85
Fortune, 89-91
Foxes, 23
Frailties, human, 109-27
Friendship, 77-80
Frogs, 35

Geese, 31-32
Goats, 23-24
God, 61-62

Hares, 28
Hawks, 32
Health, 68-70
Hearth, around the, 51-52
Herrings, 34
Homilies, miscellaneous,
    109-22
Horses, 24-26
House, around the, 51-52

Industry, 95-98
Insects, 34-35

Kites, 32

Labor, 95-98
Larks, 32
Life, 67
Lions, 26
Lobsters, 34
Love, 42-43
Luck, 89-91

Mammals, 15-29
Marriage, 43-46
Mice, 26
Misfortune, 89-91
Money, 75-77
Mules, 26

Oxen, 26

Pigs, 27
Poverty, 75-77
Priests, 62-63

Rabbits, 28

Rats, 28
Ravens, 32

Salmon, 34
Seals, 28
Sheep, 28-29
Shellfish, 34
Stupidity, 83-85
Swallows, 33

Triads, 101,106
Trout, 34

Virtue, human, 109-27

Wealth, 75-77
Wisdom, 83-85
Wolves, 29
Women, 39-42
Work, 95-98
Wrens, 33

Youth, 67-68